While the Moon Shines Bright

While the Moon Shines Bright

(a bedtime chant)

by Jeanne Whitehouse Peterson

Pictures by Margot Apple

Harper & Row, Publishers

While the Moon Shines Bright: A Bedtime Chant
Text copyright © 1981 by Jeanne Whitehouse
Illustrations copyright © 1981 by Margot Apple
All rights reserved. No part of this book may be
used or reproduced in any manner whatsoever without
written permission except in the case of brief quotations
embodied in critical articles and reviews. Printed in
the United States of America. For information address
Harper & Row, Publishers, Inc., 10 East 53rd Street,
New York, N.Y. 10022. Published simultaneously in
Canada by Fitzhenry & Whiteside Limited, Toronto.

Library of Congress Cataloging in Publication Data
Peterson, Jeanne Whitehouse.
  While the moon shines bright.

  Summary: A young child's bedtime chant about the
very last activities of the day before he hops into bed.
  [1. Bedtime—Fiction. 2. Stories in rhyme.
3. Grandfathers—Fiction] I. Apple, Margot.
II. Title.
PZ8.3.P4493Wh 1981   [E]   79-2697
ISBN 0-06-024710-X   AACR2
ISBN 0-06-024711-8 (lib. bdg.)

First Edition

to Lillian and Tom

While the Moon Shines Bright

My Granddaddy is coming,
And I hear him say:

> "Drink your milk, so cool,
> cool,
> Eat an apple,
> Jump off your stool.
>
> While the moon shines bright."

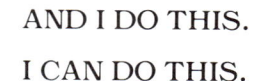

AND I DO THIS.
I CAN DO THIS.

My Granddaddy is coming,
And I hear him say:

"Wash the dishes,
Put out the cat,
Sweep the cookie crumbs under
the mat.

While the moon shines bright."

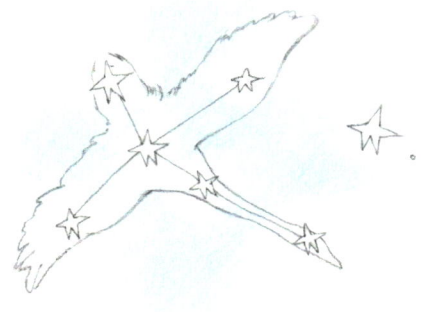

AND I DO THIS.
I CAN DO THIS.

My Granddaddy is coming,
And I hear him say:

> "Put your books in the old
> book box,
> Stack them up once,
> Then pick up your blocks.
>
> While the moon shines bright."

AND I DO THIS.
I CAN DO THIS.

My Granddaddy is coming,
And I hear him say:

> "Peek through the keyhole,
> Open the door,
> Take two giant steps,
> Rap on the floor.
>
> While the moon shines bright."

AND I DO THIS.
I CAN DO THIS.

My Granddaddy is coming,
And I hear him say:

> "Tickle the pansy on the
> window sill,
> Call to the dog running over
> the hill.
>
> While the moon shines bright."

AND I DO THIS.
I CAN DO THIS.

My Granddaddy is coming,
And I hear him say:

> "Slow down,
>   Rock on my lap awhile,
>   with me,
>   with me.
>   Tell me your story,
>   I'll tell you mine.
>
>   While the moon shines bright."

AND I DO THIS.
I CAN DO THIS.

My Granddaddy is coming,
And I hear him say:

> "Throw your clothes in the
> laundry pile,
> Brush your teeth,
> Then show me your smile.
>
> While the moon shines bright."

AND I DO THIS.
I CAN DO THIS.

My Granddaddy is coming,
And I hear him say:

> "Shut the window,
> Turn off the light.
> Pull up the blanket,
> Shut your eyes tight.
>
> While the moon shines bright."

AND I DO THIS.
I CAN DO THIS.

My Granddaddy is coming,
And I hear him whisper:

"Give me a kiss,
Wish me good night.

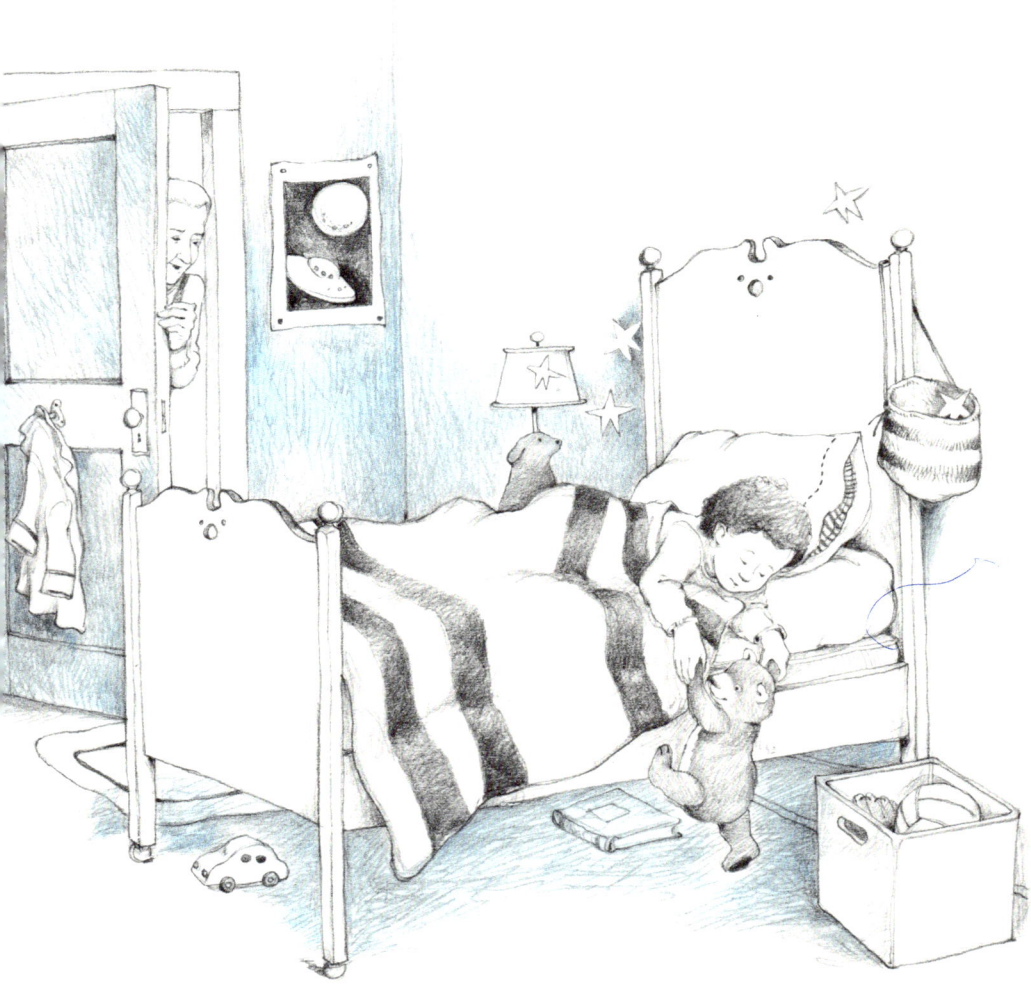

"Drink your milk, so cool,
           cool,
  Eat an apple,
  Jump off your stool.

"Wash the dishes,
 Put out the cat,
 Sweep the cookie crumbs under
        the mat.

"Put your books in the old
    book box,
  Stack them up once,
  Then pick up your blocks.

"Peek through the keyhole,
  Open the door,
  Take two giant steps,
  Rap on the floor.

"Tickle the pansy on the
    window sill,
  Call to the dog running over
    the hill.

"Slow down,
  Rock on my lap awhile
    with me,
    with me.
Tell me your story,
I'll tell you mine.

"Throw your clothes in the
   laundry pile,
Brush your teeth,
   Then show me your smile.

"Shut the window,
   Turn off the light.
Pull up the blanket
Shut your eyes tight.

"Now, give me a kiss,
 Wish me good night."

        SO I GIVE HIM A KISS
           AND WHISPER, "GOOD NIGHT."

While the moon shines bright!

✃ **Gift** ✃
Young Adult/Children's Books
Examination Center
of
Missouri State Library
Jefferson City, MO

CMSU 181-84

CHILDREN'S AND YOUNG ADULTS
BOOK EXAMINATION CENTER
MISSOURI STATE LIBRARY

523359